D1567651

INTERNET SECURITY

FROM CONCEPT TO CONSUMER

BY NEL YOMTOV

CHILDREN'S PRESS®

An Imprint of Scholastic Inc.

CONTENT CONSULTANT
Tom Patterson, Vice President of Global Security, Unisys Corporation

PHOTOGRAPHS ©: cover: Zoonar GmbH/Alamy Images; 3: Monkey Business Images/
Shutterstock, Inc.; 4 left: Reed Saxon/AP Images; 4 right: LDprod/Shutterstock, Inc.; 5 left:
bjdlzx/iStockphoto; 5 right: Charles Sykes/Invision for MasterCard/AP Images; 6: sturti/
iStockphoto; 8: The Granger Collection; 9: Emilio Segrè Visual Archives/American Institute
of Physics; 10 left: Reed Saxon/AP Images; 10 right: Courtesy of the Computer History
Museum; 11 top: Fred Prouser/Reuters; 11 bottom: Apic/Getty Images; 12: Fred Prouser/
Reuters; 13: Hermann J. Knippertz/AP Images; 14: LeFebvre Communications/EMPPL PA
Wire/AP Images; 15: Jakub Krechowicz/Shutterstock, Inc.; 16: beerkoff/Shutterstock, Inc.;
17: Zygotehaasnobrain/Shutterstock, Inc.; 18 left: Time Life Pictures/Getty Images; 18 right:
Science Source; 19 top, 19 bottom: Science and Society/Superstock, Inc.; 20: David Hecker/
Getty Images; 21: Sergei Chumakov/Thinkstock; 22: Monkey Business Images/Shutterstock,
Inc.; 24: Philippe Lopez/Getty Images; 25: Ho New/Reuters; 26: Jan Mika/Shutterstock, Inc.;
27: LDprod/Shutterstock, Inc.; 28 left: Sergio Stakhnyk/Shutterstock, Inc.; 28 right: Eugenio
Marongiu/Shutterstock, Inc.; 29 top: Peter Bernik/Shutterstock, Inc.; 29 bottom: senticus/
Shutterstock, Inc.; 30: Mel Evans/AP Images; 31: Jack Guez/Getty Images; 32: Bradley
C Bower/AP Images; 33: Gerald Herbert/AP Images; 34 left: lzf/iStockphoto; 34 right:
Bloomberg/Getty Images; 35: e X p o s e/Shutterstock, Inc.; 36: NetPics/Alamy Images;
37: Bloomberg/Getty Images; 38: Jetta Productions/Getty Images; 40: Ariel Skelley/Media
Bakery; 41: bjdlzx/iStockphoto; 42: Unisys Corp.; 44: Enigma/Alamy Images; 45: ronstik/
Shutterstock, Inc.; 46: wavebreakmedia/Shutterstock, Inc.; 47 top: Wavebreak/iStockphoto;
47 bottom: Bloomberg/Getty Images; 48: Paul King/Alamy Images; 50: Bloomberg/
Getty Images; 51: Yuri_Arcurs/iStockphoto; 52: M. Timothy O'Keefe/Alamy Images; 53
top: Bloomberg/Getty Images; 53 bottom: Paul Sakuma/AP Images; 54 left: ClassicStock/
Alamy Images; 54 right, 55 bottom: OlgaLis/Shutterstock, Inc.; 55 top: Sergey Mironov/
Shutterstock, Inc.; 56: wavebreakmedia/Shutterstock, Inc.; 57: Jim Cole/AP Images; 58
left: graytln/iStockphoto; 58 right: Gaertner/Alamy Images; 59: Charles Sykes/Invision for
MasterCard/AP Images.

LIBRARY OF CONGRESS CATALOGING-IN-PUBLICATION DATA
Yomtov, Nelson, author.
  Internet security : from concept to consumer / by Nel Yomtov.
      pages cm. — (Calling all innovators : a career for you)
  Summary: "Learn about the history of internet security and find out what it takes to make it
in this exciting career field" — Provided by publisher.
  Includes bibliographical references and index.
  ISBN 978-0-531-21896-9 (library binding : alk. paper) — ISBN 978-0-531-21914-0 (pbk.
: alk. paper)
  1. Internet — Vocational guidance — Juvenile literature. 2. Internet — Security measures —
Juvenile literature. 3. Internet — History — Juvenile literature. 4. Computer crimes — Juvenile
literature. I. Title. II. Series: Calling all innovators.
  TK5105.875.I57Y645 2015
  005.8 — dc23   2015001435

1 2 3 4 5 6 7 8 9 10 R 25 24 23 22 21 20 19 18 17 16

Science, technology, engineering, arts, and math are the fields that drive innovation. Whether they are finding ways to make our lives easier or developing the latest entertainment, the people who work in these fields are changing the world for the better. Do you have what it takes to join the ranks of today's greatest innovators? Read on to discover if a career in the exciting world of Internet security is for you.

TABLE *of* CONTENTS

Internet innovator Leonard Kleinrock displays one of the first computers ever to send a message online.

Credit card data theft is one of the most common Internet crimes.

Internet security experts routinely test computer systems to make sure they can withstand cyberattacks.

Modern mobile devices allow users to make payments without using credit cards or bank cards.

Millions of people around the world rely on the Internet for work, entertainment, and everything in between.

CHAPTER ONE

ON THE WAY TO THE WEB

Countless people rely on the Internet for even the most basic everyday tasks. They use it for work, school, shopping, communication, entertainment, and much more. Try to imagine a world where you couldn't go online. You wouldn't be able to use your laptop or tablet to research a school assignment. The only way to get in touch with faraway friends would be to mail letters or make expensive phone calls.

The Internet is a great tool, but in the wrong hands it can be a weapon. Criminal **hackers** use the Internet to steal private information, money, and more. Thankfully, Internet security experts are working hard to protect people's privacy and prevent crimes such as **data** theft and identity theft. However, with the Internet constantly growing and changing, staying a step ahead of the Web's craftiest criminals can be a tough job.

A WEB AROUND THE WORLD

1958	1969	1975	Early 1990s
Advanced Research Projects Agency (ARPA) is formed.	The first message is sent over a computer **network**.	Telenet, the world's first commercial network to use DARPANET technology, is formed.	The World Wide Web fuels the growth of the Internet.

A SUDDEN START

The first computer systems were very large. They were also expensive to build and operate. Most computers were located in government offices and at large universities and corporations. Information was sometimes sent back and forth between computers over telephone lines. The computers, however, were not part of a network. In other words, the data in one system was not available for other systems to access.

In the 1950s, political and military tensions increased between the United States and the Soviet Union. American leaders worried that the Soviets might be able to knock out U.S. military communications in the event of a war. They decided that a new type of communications network was needed to protect against such a possibility. In 1958, President Dwight D. Eisenhower created the Advanced Research Projects Agency (ARPA) to tackle this task.

The Mark II computer was built in 1947 to be used by the U.S. Navy.

J. C. R. Licklider's work at ARPA helped introduce computers and the Internet to the world.

A TEAM EFFORT

In 1962, Dr. J. C. R. Licklider of the Massachusetts Institute of Technology was placed in charge of ARPA's Information Processing Techniques Office (IPTO). During his two years in this position, Licklider assembled a team of computer scientists and researchers to develop a computer-based communications network. This linked system would allow computers to communicate with one another without going through a central hub. That way, if any part of the network was damaged, the others would still be connected.

The team worked for seven years designing and building the technology needed for such a system. Finally, on October 29, 1969, a message was successfully sent from a computer at the University of California, Los Angeles (UCLA) to one at the Stanford Research Institute in Menlo Park, California. ARPA had successfully created the world's first computer network. It was named ARPANET, short for Advanced Research Projects Agency Network.

FIRST THINGS FIRST

Leonard Kleinrock shows off the computer that made the first ARPANET connection in 1969.

"NOBODY NOTICED!"

During the early years of ARPANET, few people even knew the network existed. "In 1969, the first man landed on the moon, the Woodstock Festival took place, the Mets won the World Series . . . and the Internet was born—and nobody noticed!" ARPA computer scientist Leonard Kleinrock later said of the project.

THE ARPANET BOOM

At first, only four universities—UCLA, the Stanford Research Institute, the University of Utah, and University of California at Santa Barbara—had "host" computers hooked into ARPANET. By September 1971, 23 sites, including university and government hosts, were connected—and new host sites were hooking up each month.

The network operated on the idea that information could be transmitted electronically, computer to computer, through telephone wires in an instant. Early ARPANET users—scientists,

TELEPHONE USED TO CONNECT TO ARPANET

Internet pioneer Vinton Cerf demonstrates ARPANET in South Africa in 1974.

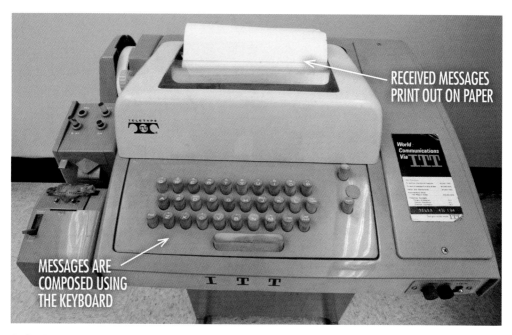

RECEIVED MESSAGES PRINT OUT ON PAPER

MESSAGES ARE COMPOSED USING THE KEYBOARD

Early ARPANET messages were composed and received using a device called a teleprinter.

professors, and the U.S. military—preferred this speedy, inexpensive form of communication to sending packages or letters through the mail. The U.S. Air Force claimed the network was "twelve times faster and cheaper" than its other communication methods.

A NETWORK OF PEOPLE

By mid-1971, ARPANET was being used for more than just scientific and military communication. Users had begun sending notes and electronic mail, or e-mail, to friends and business associates through the network. News and discussion groups began popping up as people with shared interests connected online. In 1973, other countries began to connect to ARPANET, which further expanded the reach of the new technology. ARPANET was no longer just a network of computers—it was becoming a network of people. And the best was yet to come.

This 1969 diagram shows ARPA's plans to connect computers at different sites across the country.

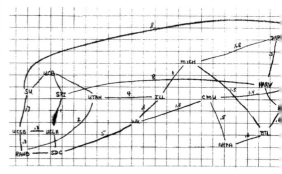

Lawrence Roberts (left) pioneered the idea of bringing ARPANET to people all around the world.

RIDING THE INFORMATION SUPERHIGHWAY

In the early 1970s, ARPA's name was changed to DARPA. The D stands for Defense. ARPANET was renamed DARPANET. Lawrence Roberts, the head of IPTO, believed the network should be more than just a tool for military research and development. He was convinced that the demand for computer communications would increase. He wanted to bring the new technology to the general public as quickly as possible.

Roberts gave his idea to the Bolt, Beranek and Newman Corporation (BBN), which had helped build ARPANET. By 1975, BBN formed a company called Telenet. Telenet built the first commercial network to make use of DARPANET technology. It provided network access to customers through telephone lines. Huge corporations and smaller organizations alike began signing up for Telenet access. The information superhighway was now open to the public.

MOVERS AND SHAKERS

Around the same time Telenet was taking off, other Internet pioneers were finding ways to expand Internet access and make it available to average users.

In 1969, Jeffrey Wilkins founded a company called CompuServe. At first, the company set up computer systems and built networks for other businesses. By the late 1970s, CompuServe was selling individual customers access to its own networks and e-mail services. During the 1990s, it was one of the most widely used Internet providers in the world.

In 1979, Duke University students Steve Bellovin and Tom Truscott created Usenet, a news exchange system between Duke and the University of North Carolina. The system operated independently of DARPANET. Students at the two schools used dial-up telephone connections to engage in online discussion groups. Eventually, people all around the world were connecting to Usenet to discuss a huge variety of topics. This service remains in use even today.

CompuServe provided Internet access to many people during the height of its success.

CREATING THE WORLD WIDE WEB

By the early 1990s, countless computers around the world were connected to what had come to be known as the Internet. Among these computers, there were millions of files available for users to access online. However, there was no easy way for the average person to sort through these files. The basic Internet tools we rely on today, such as Web browsers and search engines, did not exist yet. Though computers were connected to one another, the actual files on them were not.

Computer scientist Tim Berners-Lee helped solve this dilemma. Berners-Lee wanted to create a system that would allow Internet users to easily share and access files on the Internet, including text, images, audio, and video. He envisioned a way of navigating the Internet by linking together files on computers across the globe. He called this system the World Wide Web.

TIM BERNERS-LEE

Tim Berners-Lee was born in London, England, in 1955. After earning a degree in physics from Oxford University, he began working at CERN, the European Organization for Nuclear Research, in 1980. CERN was home to hundreds of computers. Sharing information with researchers in different locations around the globe was an important part of Berners-Lee's job. To help make this process easier, he helped create the World Wide Web, a system of files that were linked to one another using **hypertext**.

Tim Berners-Lee helped increase the popularity of the Internet by making it much easier to use.

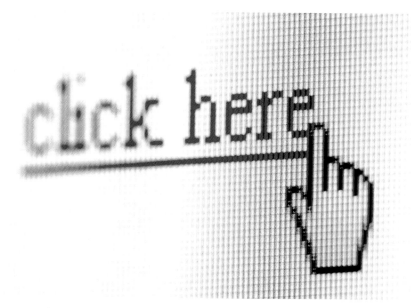

With hypertext, almost anything on the Internet can be accessed with a simple click.

THE MAGIC OF HYPERTEXT

The World Wide Web relies on the use of files called Web pages. Each page on the Web has a unique address called a uniform resource locator (URL). When a user enters a URL into a program called a Web browser, the page is displayed on-screen. From there, the user can click on hypertext links to access connected Web pages or other types of files.

Hypertext and the Web changed the way people used the Internet. Anyone with a computer and an Internet connection could post files online or browse the files posted by others. This ease of use led millions upon millions of new users to get online. Throughout the 1990s and 2000s, the Internet grew to become the sprawling global network we know today.

However, not everyone who connected to the Web had good intentions. As the Internet grew in popularity, a new type of crime became more popular as well.

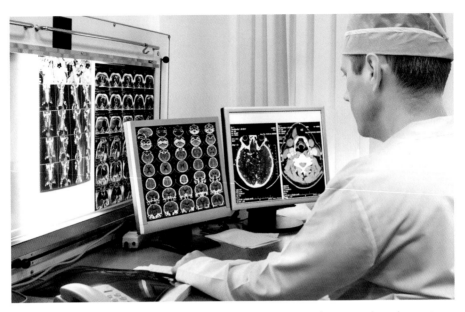

Doctors and other medical professionals rely on computers to store information about their patients.

ON GUARD

Today, people use computers to store every kind of data imaginable, from grocery lists and family photos to bank records and government secrets. If this data is held on computers that are connected to the Internet, there is a constant chance that someone, somewhere, will try to access it. The risk that valuable, confidential information could be stolen is at an all-time high.

Since the early days of the Internet, cybercriminals have found ways to use it for illegal means. Some of these crimes result in minor annoyances for victims. Others devastate people's lives. Cybercriminals are often highly skilled computer users. Some use their expertise to break into others' computers through the Internet and access files that do not belong to them. Others perform attacks on computer systems to shut them down, damage them, or even take over control. By doing these things, they can steal money, damage reputations, and much more.

INTERNET INFECTIONS

One of the most common ways for people to commit crimes online is to create and spread malicious software, or **malware**. Perhaps the most famous type of malware is the computer virus. Viruses are programs that are able to copy themselves into other programs or files. If a user downloads a virus-infected file, the other files on his or her computer can quickly become infected. Viruses can be highly destructive. Spreading from one computer to another, they can damage programs, delete files, and even cause computer hardware to malfunction.

The Trojan horse is another common type of malware. Users are tricked into installing Trojan horses by promises of useful features. Once installed, a Trojan horse program begins to fulfill its true purpose. Some Trojan horses might enable their creators to control infected computers remotely. Others might provide their creators with copies of private files from the infected computer. Unlike viruses, Trojan horses do not copy themselves into other files. They simply run silently in the background until a user notices that he or she has been hacked.

Malware infections can be extremely frustrating for computer users.

BREAKING THE CODE

During World War II (1939–1945), German forces used a machine called Enigma to protect their communications with a complex code. The device was capable of creating 158 million different code possibilities, and its settings were changed every day. This made the German code virtually unbreakable. Early in the war, Great Britain and its allies launched a secret program to break the Enigma code. This would allow them to decode Germany's messages and learn about secret plans.

Alan Turing developed a method of using electronic machines to solve incredibly complex codes.

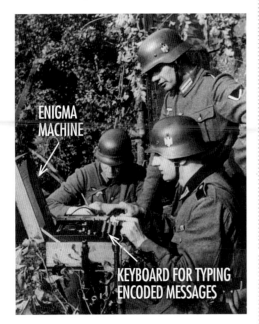

ENIGMA MACHINE

KEYBOARD FOR TYPING ENCODED MESSAGES

German soldiers use an Enigma to encode a message during World War II.

THE BOMBE THAT WON THE WAR

A team of expert code breakers, professors, writers, and puzzle solvers was assembled at Bletchley Park, a mansion in Buckinghamshire, England. British mathematician and code expert Alan Turing led the team. Turing realized that it would be almost impossible for the team to crack the code by hand. He began designing an electronic machine called the Bombe to assist in decoding Enigma messages.

The Bombe was around 7 feet (2 meters) wide and almost as tall.

As the months wore on, Turing and his associates inched ever closer to smashing the German code. Finally, in 1940, they perfected the Bombe so that it could quickly decode intercepted German messages. By breaking the code, the Allies were able to learn about German attacks ahead of time and avoid them.

TURING'S LEGACY

The Bombe was the first device of its kind. Realizing the vast potential for electronic computing devices, others began designing even more powerful machines. By 1943, British engineers had successfully created the world's first true electronic computer. Named Colossus, it was used to break a different German coding machine, as well as to solve other computational problems. These machines helped end the war and saved thousands of lives. Amazingly, the work at Bletchley Park was kept secret for more than 30 years. ✳

The Colossus computer expanded on the ideas behind Turing's Bombe.

THE WRONG KINDS OF WORMS

The type of malware known as a worm can be especially effective for hackers. Unlike viruses or Trojan horses, worms spread on their own. Users do not have to invite worms into their computers by downloading files or installing programs. Once released onto the Internet, worms can infect any computer that goes online without the proper protection in place.

A single worm can cause huge problems if it spreads far enough. In April 2004, German computer science student Sven Jaschan unleashed the Sasser worm, which targeted computers running certain Microsoft software. Sasser knocked out satellite communications at a French news agency and forced the cancellations and delays of dozens of Delta, British Airways, and Air Canada flights. The British coast guard lost its mapping service for several hours. Among other victims were universities in the United States, post offices in Taiwan, and a hospital in Sweden. The Sasser worm spread to millions of computers around the globe and caused billions of dollars in damages.

Sven Jaschan was only a teenager when he caused major problems around the world with his Sasser worm.

Botnets help hackers operate in secrecy and avoid being traced.

BUILDING A BOTNET

Much of the cybercrime waged on the Internet is conducted
by botnets. A botnet is a group of computers that hackers have
infected with malware to form a network of robot-like machines.
The hackers, called bot herders or bot masters, turn the hijacked
computers into an army of controllable bots. The robot-like army
can then be used to launch huge attacks on the bot herder's targets.

The bot herder controls the botnet remotely, making his or
her identity and location very difficult to determine. In addition,
the owners of infected bots rarely know that their computers have
been hijacked. Today, even devices such as thermostats, coffee
makers, and cars are being tricked into becoming bots. Botnets
are frequently used to spread additional malware such as spyware,
which is designed to steal sensitive information from users'
computers. Some botnets might have tens or even hundreds of
thousands of bots at work at one time.

Modern businesses rely on
the Internet to communicate
and gather information.

CHAPTER TWO

THE INTERNET AT RISK

I n less than 50 years, the Internet has grown from a simple link between a handful of universities into a massive global network. The first electronic message was sent across a network in 1969. By 2015, around 196 billion e-mails were being sent and received each day. The first Web page was created in 1991. By 2013, there were 45 trillion Web pages online, with tens of thousands more being added each day.

The Internet has grown from a community of researchers, e-mail senders, and chat room users to an indispensable tool of business and government. Some experts estimate that the number of devices connected to the Internet will increase from roughly 10 billion in 2014 to 50 billion by 2020.

The simple truth is that nearly everything we depend on in our daily lives relies on the Internet. As a result, keeping the Internet free of cybercrime is a serious economic and national security challenge.

CYBERCRIME ON THE RISE

2004	2007	2009	2013
The first worm to affect mobile devices appears.	Israel penetrates Syria's military computer networks.	The U.S. Cyber Command begins operation.	More than 13 million Americans are victims of identity theft.

Edward Snowden's leak of secret U.S. government documents made headlines around the world.

DATA BREACH BASICS

Any organization that stores information on computers must protect against the possibility of a data breach. Data breaches are security failures that lead to sensitive or confidential information being viewed, stolen, or used by someone not authorized to do so. They can occur in many different ways. Simple human error is the most common cause of data breaches. An employee might lose or misplace a laptop, smartphone, or flash drive that holds confidential information. Such data might include names, e-mail and home addresses, Social Security and credit card numbers, and medical records.

Some data breaches occur when a user accesses documents or alters or deletes data from a system without authorization. For example, in 2013, National Security Agency (NSA) employee Edward Snowden leaked tens of thousands of classified U.S. government documents to the media. The documents revealed details about a global **surveillance** operation run by the NSA. Snowden fled to Russia to avoid criminal charges for his actions in the United States.

CYBERCRIMINALS AT WORK

An ever-increasing form of data breach occurs when cybercriminals hack into computer systems to steal information. In 2006, the U.S. Department of Veterans Affairs (VA) reported that a laptop containing the private information of more than 26 million people had been stolen. The laptop was found a month later with the data intact, but it is impossible to know whether the information was accessed or copied. The VA paid $20 million to settle a lawsuit filed by veterans whose information appeared in the stolen files.

In 2009, hackers broke into the computers of Heartland Payment Systems, a credit card processing company. The hackers stole the names and account numbers of around 100 million credit card and debit card owners. One year later, the mastermind behind the hacking scheme was sentenced to 20 years in prison. The attack cost Heartland $140 million in fines and payments to the victims.

Hacker Albert Gonzalez led an attack on Heartland Payment Systems in 2009.

IDENTITY THEFT

Sometimes hackers use information stolen in data breaches to commit a crime called identity theft. Using stolen credit card information to purchase things is one form of identity theft. In more serious instances, a criminal can steal someone's personal information and actually assume his or her identity.

One common technique hackers use to steal personal information is called **phishing**. Phony e-mails are created to look like they come from reputable institutions such as banks or credit card companies and are sent to unsuspecting victims. The messages ask the targets to confirm passwords, Social Security numbers, and other confidential information. Unaware the e-mails are bogus, many people provide the requested information to the thieves without thinking twice.

A hacker group in China was reported to have used phishing schemes to steal data from more than 100 U.S. companies from 2006 to 2013. The hackers used the data to break into the systems of companies involved in telecommunications, energy, media, financial services, and other industries. They then stole information relating to manufacturing procedures, business plans, and new technologies, as well as the confidential e-mails of high-ranking employees.

Phishing schemes often target the elderly, who tend to be inexperienced Internet users.

Although many banks and credit card companies offer protection from identity theft, it remains a major problem.

SHAMELESS CRIMINALS

An identity thief can damage a victim's reputation or cause financial ruin. A hacker who gets into your Facebook or Twitter account can send malware or phishing links to your friends. A hacked e-mail account can allow someone to broadcast your most private messages and photos across the Internet. If a hacker uses your stolen Social Security number in a dishonest deal, you may be held responsible. Victims of identity theft are often denied loans, credit, and access to government services because their financial reputation has been damaged.

Identity theft is the fastest-growing crime in the United States. According to one report, 13.1 million Americans were victims in 2013. Thieves have been known to go on wild spending sprees, rent apartments, and even purchase homes and cars. They have used stolen information to obtain medical care and student financial aid, drain bank accounts, and even file fake tax returns. Worst of all, identity thieves are very difficult to track down and bring to justice.

MODERN MARVELS

With cloud computing, people no longer need storage devices to access their files.

UP IN THE CLOUD

One of the fastest-growing computer technologies is called cloud computing. Users of cloud services store their files on remote **servers** instead of their own computers. This enables them to access their files from any online-enabled device at any time. As long as they can connect to the Internet, they can pull their information out of the "cloud." Some cloud services even offer the ability to run entire programs from the cloud without installing software on the device itself. Users can create spreadsheets, edit photos, and more from inside their Web browsers.

A MATTER OF TRUST

Storing files in the cloud offers many advantages. Users who own multiple computers do not have to think about which files are stored on which machine. They don't have to worry about leaving important files on home or office computers while traveling, and they don't have to use hard drives or other storage devices to transport files to different places. Cloud services also make it easy for multiple people to collaborate and share files together.

Because people use the cloud to host a variety of valuable and private data, they must be able to trust that their files will be safe on a cloud service company's servers.

Cloud computing allows users to easily access the same files across many different devices.

As a result, companies that offer cloud services must protect their servers using the latest Internet security technology.

CLOUD-BASED ANTIVIRUS TECHNOLOGY

Many computer users rely on antivirus software and other programs to keep their systems free of malware. However, with new types of malware being created constantly, such software only works if it is updated regularly. Cloud-based security software is making it easier than ever to ensure that users are protected from the latest threats. Such programs do not need to be updated. Instead, the information about different types of malware is stored in the cloud. The user's computer simply connects to the remote server to access the data it needs to detect

Cloud services enable users to access their files from anywhere they have Internet access.

threats. Cloud-based security software not only spares users from having to constantly perform updates, it also provides access to the latest protection methods within minutes of their availability. ✳

Cloud companies store users' files in huge rooms filled with servers.

The Internet is an important part of modern military communications.

NATIONAL SECURITY AND CYBERWARFARE

Though the Internet has grown far beyond its original purpose as a tool for the military, it is today playing a bigger role than ever in the way wars are fought. Militaries around the world employ hackers to launch cyberattacks and spy on the activities of enemies and potential threats—who, in turn, also maintain their own state-of-the-art Internet security systems.

Unlike the damage caused by a rifle or a bomb, cyberattacks are designed to disrupt government and military computer networks. Attacks on these systems might ultimately cause physical damage to a nation's armies or **infrastructure**. For example, cyberattacks could potentially be used to shut down a country's power grid, plunging the nation into darkness. Combating cyberattacks is no easy task. They are difficult to predict, and it is often difficult to identify who is behind the attacks.

MILITARY MALWARE

Cyberattacks can be especially effective when used in combination with traditional military activities. In 2006, Israeli secret agents snuck into the hotel room of a Syrian government official and installed malware on his laptop that would allow them to monitor his communications. When the Israelis examined files on the laptop's hard drive, they realized Syria was secretly building a facility to construct a nuclear bomb. The Israelis feared the Syrians would use the bomb against them.

In September 2007, the Israelis launched an air attack that destroyed the nuclear facility. The Israeli jets managed to slip past Syria's radar defenses without detection. But how? The Israelis had unleashed malware that attacked the Syrian military's computer networks. The program knocked out the entire Syrian radar system while the raid was taking place. It is believed the cyberattack on Syria's network may have been conducted from computers carried on board the Israeli jets.

Today, fighter planes and other military vehicles can launch cyberattacks in addition to physical attacks.

CYBERTERRORISM

National militaries aren't the only groups using the Internet to wage war today. Modern terrorist groups are frequently turning to the Internet to launch attacks on their enemies. "The cyberterrorism threat is real, and it is rapidly expanding," said Robert S. Mueller III, former director of the Federal Bureau of Investigation (FBI), in 2012. "Terrorists have shown a clear interest in pursuing hacking skills."

Just like government-employed hackers, cyberterrorists often target the computer systems used to operate a foe's infrastructure. The FBI warns that possible targets of cyberterrorism include communications systems, electricity grids, and banks. Nuclear plants and emergency services such as police, firefighters, and rescue personnel are also at risk. Successful attacks on these targets could be devastating—especially if the attacks are combined with physical attacks and further cyberattacks.

Cyberattacks on nuclear power plants could leave huge areas with no electricity.

President Obama has made protecting the country from cyberattacks a priority.

FIGHTING CYBERATTACKS

"Cyberspace is real," President Barack Obama stated at a news conference in May 2009. "And so are the risks that come with it." In the same speech, the president listed numerous cyber threats that could harm Americans: a lone hacker, an industrial spy, foreign intelligence services, and others. These examples illustrated the point that anyone with an Internet connection and the right training can launch a cyberattack.

In response to this threat, President Obama announced the creation of the U.S. Cyber Command, a new White House office led by a cybersecurity coordinator to ensure that the nation's computer networks are "secure, trustworthy, and resilient." Cyber Command's mission is to protect military computer networks and conduct offensive cyberattacks against unfriendly forces.

FROM THIS TO THAT

SECURITY ON THE GO

Until the late 2000s, almost all personal computing was done using desktop or laptop computers. As a result, cybercriminals focused their energy primarily on these kinds of machines. However, as smartphones, tablets, and other portable devices have become more popular, hackers have begun to see them as valuable targets. In recent years, there has been a regular stream of malware specifically targeting mobile devices.

It is helpful to learn about a device's security features before making a purchase.

WIRELESS WORMS

Cabir, the first worm to target mobile phones, appeared in 2004. Since then, it has spread around the world. Once it has installed itself on a phone, it uses the device's Bluetooth wireless signals to spread itself to other nearby devices. Though the worm does not cause major issues for infected phones, its appearance stood as a warning that malware could target phones just as it does other online-enabled devices.

Mobile malware can cause confusion for smartphone users.

MOBILE MALWARE

The effects of mobile malware vary. In some cases, it can simply be an annoyance. For example, the Skuller Trojan horse replaces system icons with a skull icon. Some mobile malware can be a bigger problem. For instance, a mobile Trojan horse might secretly send expensive text messages, resulting in a surprisingly large phone bill for the infected device's owner. The worst mobile malware is even capable of stealing confidential data stored on a device.

STAYING UP-TO-DATE

Today, most mobile device manufacturers offer users three key security features: anti-malware software, utilities for locating a stolen phone and remotely locking or wiping its data, and data **encryption**. Some devices also allow users to block calls and messages from strangers. Security experts suggest that mobile device users update their anti-malware software regularly and remain wary of any app, e-mail attachment, or other download that does not come from a trusted source. ☀

Some mobile malware can transmit itself to nearby devices using wireless connections.

Modern operating systems have basic virus protection features built in.

VIRUS PROTECTION

The first documented removal of a computer virus was performed by German computer security expert Bernd Fix in 1987. Since then, many effective and easy-to-use tools have been developed in the fight against cybercrime, ranging from high-tech security software for organizations to simpler programs for average computer users. One of the most essential tools for any computer is antivirus software. Antivirus programs detect, prevent, and remove viruses, worms, and other malware from a computer. They do this by searching the computer's hard drive and incoming files for potential threats to the system. This is a simple, inexpensive way to protect against common threats.

Many experts agree that antivirus programs play only a small part in detecting malware. As more viruses and other malware are released, users must continually update their antivirus software and other protections to keep them effective against new threats.

OTHER WAYS TO STAY SAFE

Antivirus programs are not the only tools used in the fight against cybercrime. Another popular form of protection is known as a firewall. A firewall is a program, physical device, or combination of both that is installed in a computer or computer network. Its job is to block viruses and other malware from getting through. A firewall is programmed to allow only data that meets specific standards into the computer. Any data that does not meet these standards is denied access. Computer owners or network administrators can adjust the firewall's settings to meet their specific security needs, with the newest firewalls even protecting information on mobile devices and in the cloud.

Encryption is another way of protecting data from hackers. Encrypted data works like a message that has been translated into secret code. Only computers with the right tools and keys to decode the data can read it. For example, when someone enters a credit card number to purchase something from an online store, the data is encrypted as it travels to the store's servers. This helps protect it from being stolen along the way by hackers.

Different kinds of software offer different security features to users.

A company's security workers might spend part of their time teaching other employees how to keep their systems secure.

CHAPTER THREE

ON THE JOB

A s businesses and governments around the globe continue to invest heavily in cybersecurity, the need for qualified computer security specialists is growing. According to one report, the demand for cybersecurity professionals has grown more than three and a half times faster than the demand for other information technology (IT) jobs. It has also increased 12 times faster than the demand for all other non-IT jobs. In fact, there are so many Internet security jobs available that there aren't enough workers to fill them. Current worker shortages are estimated to be between 20,000 and 40,000, with the lack of qualified pros likely to continue for years. This means there is plenty of room for newcomers who want to make a difference by protecting the world's computer systems from thieves, terrorists, and other cybercriminals.

INTERNATIONAL HEADLINES

2012	2013	2014
The U.S. government hacks into Web sites run by the terrorist organization Al-Qaeda.	Chinese hackers attack the computer systems of the New York Times.	U.S. officials accuse North Korea of hacking into computers of Sony Pictures Entertainment.

LEARNING THE TRADE

There are many types of jobs available in cybersecurity, from entry-level positions at small companies to high-responsibility roles such as the director of a national government's cybersecurity. Each requires specific education, training, and experience.

One reason there is such a need for good cybersecurity experts is that the field is constantly growing and changing. Hackers are always working on new methods of attacking their victims. As a result, security professionals must be able to learn and adapt quickly. This means that education is a never-ending process for many people in the field. They must always remain up-to-date on the latest technological advances, as well as on the activities of cybercriminals operating in the darkest corners of the Internet. With the level of expertise required and the sometimes stressful nature of the job, cybersecurity might not be for everyone. However, for the right kind of person, it can be a highly rewarding career.

High school, college (pictured below), and online computer classes are a good way to learn the basic skills needed for Internet security jobs.

Information security analysts must ensure that an organization's servers are always protected from the latest threats.

INFORMATION SECURITY ANALYST

Like most workers in cybersecurity, information security analysts work for governments, military, businesses, nonprofit organizations, financial institutions, oil and utility companies, and other groups. These professionals install and operate software such as firewalls and encryption programs on their employers' computers and networks. Security analysts also conduct penetration tests. These are simulated malware attacks that can reveal possible weaknesses in computer systems before a real attack can occur.

In the event of an actual attack, information security analysts also play the role of detective. They investigate data breaches and prepare reports that explain the extent of the damage caused and how it can be corrected.

Information security analyst jobs usually require at least a bachelor's degree in computer science or computer programming. In addition, analysts may need to show experience dealing with specific types of security issues or equivalent training from military experience.

AN INTERVIEW WITH CYBERSECURITY EXPERT TOM PATTERSON

Tom Patterson is vice president of global security at Unisys Corporation. He has provided security for space shuttle and aircraft carrier launches. He has also protected oil rigs, banks, and hospitals from terrorists, organized criminals, and foreign intelligence services.

When did you start thinking about a career in cybersecurity? What was it that inspired you? Back when I got started in cybersecurity, there wasn't a career path to even think about. Security was just forms being filled out by secretaries. Security wasn't even an issue for most. I was always fascinated by figuring out how things worked. At one job, I was issued a black box called a KG-84 that could allow me to send a message that only my bosses could read. Taking it apart and seeing the amazing things at work inside the box made me want to learn about this new science of cybersecurity.

What kinds of classes did you take in school and beyond to prepare for your career? In middle school, the teacher that made the most impact was Mr. Griffin's seventh-grade math class. He not only taught me math, but also taught me logic and how to think. In college, my major was information systems management, which provided a great overview for how both computers and software worked. In cybersecurity, it's critical that you understand how phones, computers, and networks actually work, so you can get to work defending them.

What other jobs and skills prepared you for your cybersecurity career? My first job was as a **negotiator**, which had nothing to do with cybersecurity, except for one thing: I was often sent to parts of the world that had wars and other dangerous conflicts going on, so I used cybersecurity equipment that helped me communicate securely and stay safe. My job also requires strong communication skills. The best cybersecurity folks . . . [are able to] not only do it, but also explain it.

Do you have a particular project that you're especially proud of or one that really took your career to another level? When computer viruses were very new, I discovered that a new one was trying to infect a space shuttle about to launch. When I notified NASA [National Aeronautics and Space Administration], they let me into the Kennedy Space Center in Florida to ensure that their mission computers were safe. Knowing I helped prevent something bad from happening helped make me very passionate about wanting to use cybersecurity to make the world a safer place.

It must take an entire team to handle cybersecurity functions. How important is the ability to work as part of a team in your job? Living and working internationally and often in war zones teaches the wisdom of working in teams. Everybody is better at some things than others, and a good team will put the right people in the right positions. The result is greater than the sum of its parts.

Is there a specific field in which you do most of your work? I'm very focused on the area of critical infrastructure protection. This is where normal companies such as banks or water or power companies come under attack by entire countries or global organized crime gangs. The companies' computers are often overmatched by the amount of technical sophistication thrown at them in cyberattacks. I work with governments and security companies focused on defending these companies to level the playing field.

What advice would you give to a young person who wants to enter the field of cybersecurity? This is the best time in history to start a career in cybersecurity, and the younger you start, the better you'll be. Learn how your devices work. Learn how to write a program and start making something online, like a Web page, a game, or an app. Once you do, there are great careers ahead, working with moral and ethical people in both government and in private industry. ✳

Investigators may take computers from crime scenes so they can be analyzed in a lab.

INFORMATION SECURITY FORENSICS INVESTIGATOR

Information security crime investigators often work for police departments, private investigation firms, insurance companies, and government agencies such as the FBI. A security crime investigator analyzes computer systems to gain information that might help solve a crime. This might include inspecting a hacked computer system to find out how its security was breached. It might also include examining a computer that has been used to commit crimes, in order to help track down the criminal. Such computers might also contain hidden information that can be used in a criminal trial. Crime investigators write reports that will later be used in court and may also testify at trials. In addition to a college degree, certifications such as Certified Computer Forensics Examiner (CCFE) or Certified Penetration Tester (CPT) are usually required for this job.

SECURITY SOFTWARE DEVELOPER

Network security software developers are responsible for designing and building new security systems. Creating firewalls, antivirus programs, and data encryption methods are important parts of the job. Developers come up with ideas for fighting against new attacks and use these ideas to plan new software features. Once they have an idea of what they want to do, they work closely with computer programmers to bring their vision to life. As a result, they need a solid understanding of programming languages.

Testing and modifying the software is also part of a developer's job. Like security analysts, they often simulate attacks on computer systems to determine weak spots through which a real hacker might gain entrance. Based on their findings, they write reports to explain how well the system's security software performs.

A bachelor's degree in computer science is typically required to begin a career as a software developer. Understanding the security development process and gaining certifications are also helpful. Communication skills are highly valued because many security software developers must train others and write about technical topics for many different audiences.

Software developers spend a lot of time working with computer code.

THE ARTISTIC SIDE

Graphic designers put a lot of thought into choosing the right colors for a program's interface.

WHERE SOFTWARE MEETS ITS USER

When you load up an antivirus program or open the control panel for your computer's firewall software, you don't see the computer code that the software is built on. Instead, you are presented with the program's user **interface** (UI). This is an arrangement of text, graphics, menus, and other elements that you can use to issue commands and receive information from the program. Interfaces are created by teams of creative thinkers whose job is to make software both visually appealing and easy to use.

DESIGNING AN INTERACTION

UI designers determine how information is laid out on-screen and organized in menus, as well as how users input information. There are almost limitless options to consider in this process. What should happen when a user right clicks on a menu option? Where will the program's main navigation buttons be placed? Should the program make a noise when it is done scanning for viruses?

UI designers must think about their program's intended use as they work. Is it a simple antivirus program for everyday use

Designers work together to make programs as attractive and easy to use as possible.

most important parts of graphic design is typography, or working with fonts and letter spacing. Playing with the scale and size of graphic elements is also critical in creating balanced designs. Many graphic designers repeat the same colors or shapes within a project to tie individual elements together. ✳

Designers also create packaging designs to help their programs stand out on store shelves.

or a complex firewall to protect the network of a major corporation? Does the program have many different options and features, or does it only perform a few basic tasks? The answers to these and other questions can have a major effect on how a program's interface is designed.

VISUAL APPEAL

UI designers work closely with graphic designers and other visual artists to give an interface an attractive, effective appearance. Graphic designers work with colors, shapes, lines, textures, and space. Sometimes they might use photographs and illustrations to instruct users how the software works. One of the

Banks rely on Internet-connected computer systems to store customers' financial information.

CHAPTER FOUR

RESPONDING TO A CYBERATTACK

n July 2014, a cyberattack on the United States' largest bank, JPMorgan Chase, **compromised** the accounts of 76 million homes and 7 million businesses. Operating overseas, the hackers stole the names, addresses, phone numbers, and e-mail addresses of account holders. In the wake of this massive data breach, JPMorgan announced plans to spend $250 million on cybersecurity each year.

The attack on JPMorgan showed that even the world's largest banking institutions are at risk of being harmed by cybercrime. Even worse, the disaster was not an isolated incident. Statistics indicate that cybercrime is ramping up faster than Internet security pros can keep up with. In other words, cyberattacks are bound to happen from time to time no matter how much security is in place. When they do, the victims must act swiftly. A quick, focused response is the key to limiting the theft of sensitive confidential data.

DISASTROUS DATA BREACHES

2009	2011	2014
Heartland Payment Systems is hacked, resulting in one of the largest Internet data breaches to date.	Personal information is stolen from about 77 million people when Sony's PlayStation Network is hacked.	The online auction site eBay is hacked, affecting personal data of most of its 145 million members.

THE ATTACK BEGINS

Nancy is the owner of Test Prepper, a provider of test preparation courses and materials, including online classes. One morning at work, Nancy went online and saw a message directed to her on the company's Web site. "I've hacked your system," said the message. "If you don't give me $250,000, I will expose the personal information of your customers."

Although this attack is fictional, similar hijackings of sensitive data occur every day. Let's see how Nancy responded to her system's security breach.

Nancy quickly called a meeting with the company's top officers and the director of the IT department. Though they realized the threatening message could be a hoax, they decided to take the Web site offline to be safe. All of the company's 60,000 digital files were transferred to another system.

Michael Daniel is one of the nation's leading experts on cybersecurity.

MICHAEL DANIEL, CYBERSECURITY CZAR

Michael Daniel is the U.S. cybersecurity coordinator. Daniel leads the development and implementation of the country's cybersecurity plans and policies. In addition, he ensures that the federal government works together with private businesses and other nations to protect the United States and its allies from cyberattack. Before he was named cybersecurity coordinator, Daniel served for 12 years as the chief of the intelligence branch, national security division, where he oversaw classified Department of Defense programs.

A cyberattack can have a serious impact on a company of any size.

CALLING IN THE PROFESSIONALS

Nancy knew the attack on Test Prepper's system could cause irreparable damage to the business. She decided to hire a team of professional system breach specialists to help deal with the situation. These technicians performed a complete examination of Test Prepper's computer network: servers, software, network security, and firewalls. After hours of work, the team discovered a Trojan horse that had been unleashed on the system by the hacker. Now knowing the nature of the attack, the technicians were able to eliminate the Trojan in about 10 hours.

Before returning the company's files to the cleaned system, the technicians installed new security software on it and changed all employee passwords to help prevent a similar attack in the future.

Symantec's Norton AntiVirus is one of the most widely used Internet security programs.

THE SYMANTEC CORPORATION

The Symantec Corporation is one of the world's largest security software manufacturers. Headquartered in Mountain View, California, Symantec makes and sells the popular Norton brand of consumer security products, as well as a wide range of other products and services aimed at businesses and other organizations.

A GROWING BUSINESS

Symantec was founded in 1982 by Gary Hendrix to work on programs related to artificial intelligence. In 1990, it merged with the highly successful software company Peter Norton Computing. Norton specialized in programs that back up files, check for viruses, and restore lost data in computer systems. Within three years, Norton products made up more than 80 percent of Symantec's total revenue. Today, Symantec has more than 18,500 employees in more than 50 countries. Individual consumers and small businesses, as well as the largest international corporations and governments use Symantec's products and data storage and security services.

SAFE SALES

Symantec products are used by many businesses to prevent point-of-sale (POS) data breaches. POS systems are the in-store systems where customers pay merchants for products or services. Some POS dealings are carried out using cash, but most payments are made when customers swipe credit or debit cards through a card reader device. Attacks on POS setups are common. Attackers use malware to intercept card data as it is being sent over the Internet to the banks and credit card companies that process payments.

Symantec's headquarters is located in Mountain View, California.

AN UNEXPECTED ATTACK

Even as a leader in the field of Internet security, Symantec has itself been a victim of cyberattacks. In 2012, the company announced that its own network had been hacked through a server operated by the government of India. The company reported that only outdated information had been hijacked and that the hacker stole no customer information. ✳

Symantec offers a wide range of security software.

Some older modems used telephones to connect to the Internet.

CONNECTING THROUGH THE PHONE

In the early years of the Web, dial-up Internet access was the only way users were able to go online. Dial-up connections to the Internet are made through the user's telephone lines and a device called a modem. A modem changes the form of electric signals so that information can be sent through telephone lines from one computer to another. To go online, the user's computer dials a telephone number that connects to an Internet service provider (ISP). The ISP grants the user's computer an Internet protocol (IP) address and the connection is made. When the online session is over, the call is ended, and the user's computer is no longer connected to the Internet. The next time the user goes online, a new call is made and a different IP address is provided to that computer. Establishing a dial-up connection takes time. A user can wait anywhere from several seconds to a couple of minutes before being online, depending on location and the type of data being transmitted.

NOT SO FAST

In 2000, 34 percent of American adults used dial-up connections to get online. By 2013, that number had decreased to 2

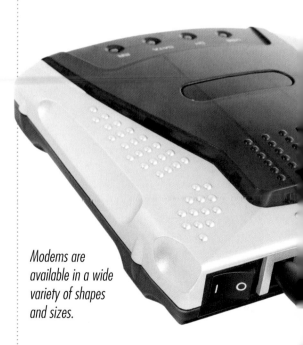

Modems are available in a wide variety of shapes and sizes.

Modern Internet connections make it possible for people to use the telephone and go online at the same time.

percent. But even though dial-up connections are no longer very popular, they are the only way some people can go online. Most dial-up users live in regions where broadband Internet access is unavailable, such as rural or remote areas. A broadband connection typically transfers data 10 to 20 times faster than dial-up. For example, a music file that takes 20 seconds to download using a broadband connection may take as long as 18 minutes to download through a dial-up connection.

PHONE LINE CONNECTS TO INTERNET

CABLE CONNECTS TO COMPUTER

A SMALL UPSIDE TO SLOW SPEEDS

Although dial-up services are slow and less convenient than more modern methods of connecting to the Internet, they do have one advantage. With broadband connections, your computer is always online. Unless there is a problem, its connection to the Internet is never broken. This makes your computer's IP address more vulnerable to hackers than the ever-changing IP addresses of a dial-up user. Therefore, it can be more difficult for hackers to gain access to a computer that uses a dial-up connection to go online. ✳

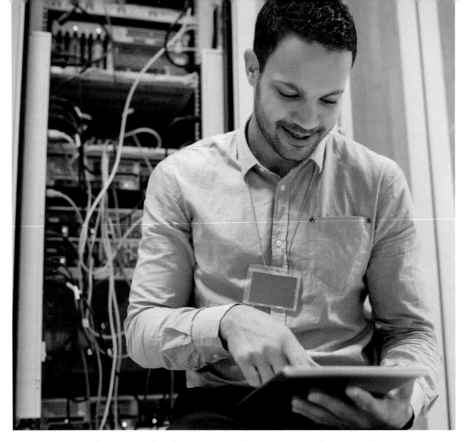

Security experts perform tests on breached systems to determine how hackers were able to gain access.

DELIVERING THE BAD NEWS

Once Nancy and her team were confident that the data breach
was fixed and the network security was improved, the Test Prepper
Web site was put back online. While Nancy had let all of her users
know there had been an attack, she now had to inform them that
their personal data had been compromised. Nancy wrote a personal
message to her customers and posted it on the company's site. She
explained that the company's network had been hacked but that no
critical information—such as credit card numbers or Social Security
numbers—had been taken. Nancy offered her customers discounts
on Test Prepper products and services as an apology. In the end,
the company lost some of its customers, but most appreciated the
company's honesty and were willing to forgive them for the incident.

SEARCHING FOR A SUSPECT

With the threat over, Nancy wanted to find out who had committed the crime. She called the local police, who sent information security crime investigators out to inspect Test Prepper's systems and ask some questions. The investigators promised Nancy that they would do everything they could to find the hacker, but they also warned her that there was no guarantee that this person would be brought to justice.

Cybercrime isn't going away anytime soon. With the vast amount of valuable information stored on computers, hackers will always search for new ways to commit crimes online. The only thing to do is keep fighting against them every step of the way. Computer users must remain vigilant about keeping their data safe, and security professionals must continually invent new kinds of protection. It will be a difficult battle, and it will take a lot of very skilled computer experts to win. Are you up to the challenge?

Police departments rely on their Internet security experts to help solve cybercrimes.

THE FUTURE

With mounting fears over hacking and terrorism, the global cybersecurity market is growing by leaps and bounds. Much of the growth is due to increased security devoted to cloud computing and mobile devices. Hundreds of new security businesses are expected to crop up all around the world to develop and implement new technologies to combat cybercrime.

TOUCH SCREEN DISPLAYS DATA AND ALLOWS USERS TO MAKE ADJUSTMENTS TO SMART DEVICE

Fingerprint scanners can add a new layer of security to mobile devices.

Place Your Finger

Lift and rest your finger on the Home button repeatedly.

BUTTON IS ALSO A FINGERPRINT SCANNER

Refrigerators are some of the many devices that technology companies are working to connect to the Internet.

EVERYTHING IS CONNECTED

Technology companies are working to bring our cars, homes, businesses, and even our bodies online. In the near future, everything from coffee makers and fitness equipment to air-conditioning systems, toilets, and baby monitors will be connected to the Internet. This will allow users to manage their homes remotely using computers or mobile devices. However, the more connected our technology becomes, the greater the risk that hackers will be able to cause problems. Many companies are currently working on products that will safeguard Internet-connected home devices from attacks.

TOUCH AND GO

No two fingerprints are alike. That reality has produced a promising new development in Internet security: fingerprint-scanning technology. This technology enables devices to read an image of a person's fingerprint and confirm that it belongs to the authorized user of the device. For example, recent models of Apple's iPhone have included mobile fingerprint-scanning devices. Developers hope the new technology will replace passwords and identification numbers as gateways for logging into accounts and paying for things.

However, while fingerprint scanning may offer a new level of security, it has risks of its own. Some users are concerned that storing records of their fingerprints online will allow hackers to steal the data and commit identity theft.

THE WEB WIDENS

Even today, the Internet continues to grow. As the technology needed to get online becomes cheaper and easier to install, usage spreads into areas where it was not previously common. From 2000 to 2014, for example, Internet usage in Africa increased by nearly 6,500 percent! In the same period, usage went up by 3,300 percent in the Middle East and more than 1,600 percent in Latin America and the Caribbean. As more people go online, more computers must be protected and more cybercriminals are born. The rising use of the Web will no doubt keep security professionals busy for decades to come. ✸

Some businesses allow users to pay through their smartphones, eliminating the need for physical credit cards.

CAREER STATS

INFORMATION SECURITY ANALYSTS

MEDIAN ANNUAL SALARY (2012): $86,170

NUMBER OF JOBS (2012): 75,100

PROJECTED JOB GROWTH (2012–2022): 37%, much faster than average

PROJECTED INCREASE IN JOBS (2012–2022): 27,400

REQUIRED EDUCATION: Bachelor's degree in a field related to computer or information science

NETWORK AND COMPUTER SYSTEMS ADMINISTRATORS

MEDIAN ANNUAL SALARY (2012): $72,560

NUMBER OF JOBS (2012): 366,400

PROJECTED JOB GROWTH (2012–2022): 12%, as fast as average

PROJECTED INCREASE IN JOBS (2012–2022): 42,900

REQUIRED EDUCATION: Bachelor's degree in a field related to computer or information science

DATABASE ADMINISTRATORS

MEDIAN ANNUAL SALARY (2012): $77,080

NUMBER OF JOBS (2012): 118,700

PROJECTED JOB GROWTH (2012–2022): 15%, faster than average

PROJECTED INCREASE IN JOBS (2012–2022): 17,900

REQUIRED EDUCATION: Bachelor's degree in a field related to computer or information science; most
database administrators typically have work experience in a related field

Figures reported by the United States Bureau of Labor Statistics

RESOURCES

BOOKS

Bonnice, Sherry. *Computer Programmer.* Broomall, PA: Mason Crest, 2014.

Colt, James P. *Cyberpredators.* New York: Chelsea House, 2011.

Cunningham, Kevin. *Computer Graphics.* New York: Children's Press, 2013.

Hynes, Patricia Freeland. *Cyber Cop.* Ann Arbor, MI: Cherry Lake, 2007.

Mara, Wil. *Information Security Analyst.* Ann Arbor, MI: Cherry Lake, 2013.

Yomtov, Nel. *Internet Inventors.* New York: Children's Press, 2013.

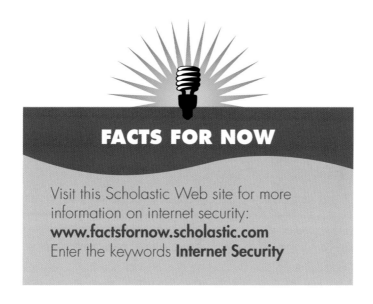

FACTS FOR NOW

Visit this Scholastic Web site for more information on internet security:
www.factsfornow.scholastic.com
Enter the keywords **Internet Security**

GLOSSARY

compromised (KAHM-pruh-mized) exposed to danger

data (DAY-tuh) information collected in a place so that something can be done with it

encryption (en-KRIP-shun) the conversion of data into coded information that requires the correct key or software to decode

hackers (HA-kurz) people who are experts at accessing and making changes to computer systems

hypertext (HYE-pur-tekst) text or other objects on a Web page that link to other pages or files when clicked

infrastructure (IN-fruh-struk-chur) the basic facilities necessary for a community to function, including power lines and water systems

interface (IN-tur-fase) the point at which two things meet; for example, a keyboard is one type of interface between a user and a computer

malware (MAL-wair) software that is intended to damage, disable, or infiltrate computer systems

negotiator (ni-GOH-shee-ate-ur) a person who tries to reach an agreement by discussing something

network (NET-wurk) a group of connected computers or computer equipment

phishing (FISH-ing) the activity of trying to steal information by tricking people into providing it themselves

servers (SUR-vurz) the main computers in a network that provide files and service that are used by the other computers

surveillance (sur-VAY-luhns) observation of a place or person in order to gain information

INDEX

Page numbers in *italics* indicate illustrations.

INDEX *(CONTINUED)*

ABOUT THE AUTHOR

NEL YOMTOV is an award-winning author with a passion for writing nonfiction books for young readers. He has written books and graphic novels about history, geography, science, and other subjects.

Nel has worked at Marvel Comics, where he edited, wrote, and colored hundreds of titles. He has also served as editorial director of a children's book publisher and as publisher of Hammond World Atlas books.

Yomtov lives in the New York City area with his wife, Nancy, a teacher. His son, Jess, is a sports journalist.